WHAT IS THIS? The book of me! Every thumbprint on the page shows who I saw and what made my day. If it's lost, return it please! My name is here, as you will see.

MY LIFE IN THUMBPRINTS

An Inky Autobiography

By The Small Object and You

CHRONICLE BOOKS

DRAWING AND ACTIVITY PAGES

A record for birthdays, wardrobes, travel, quotes, and portraits.

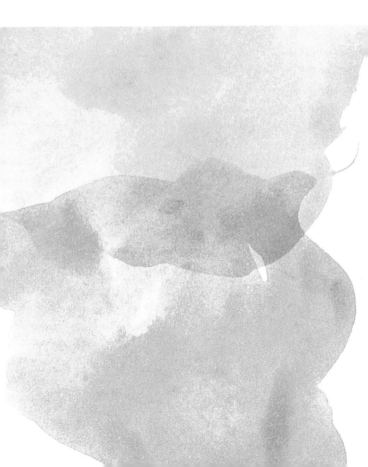

Age

Age

Age

Age

Age

Age

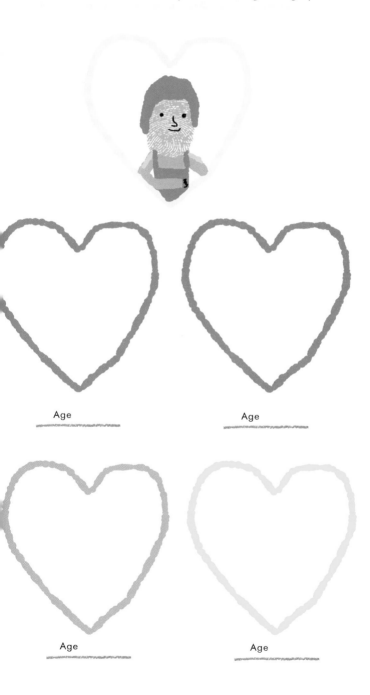

Age

Age

Age

Age

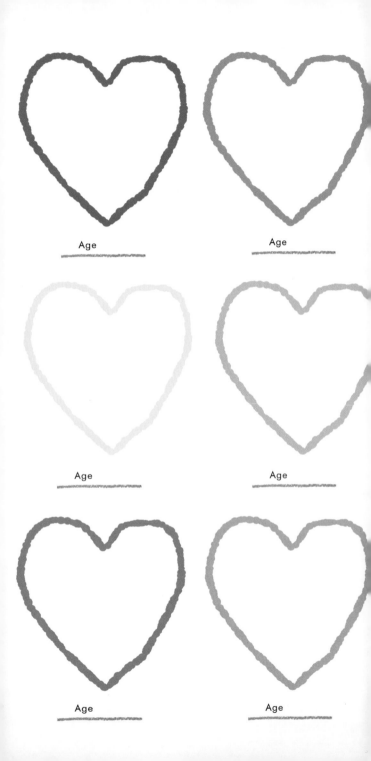

Age

Age

Age

Age

Age

Age

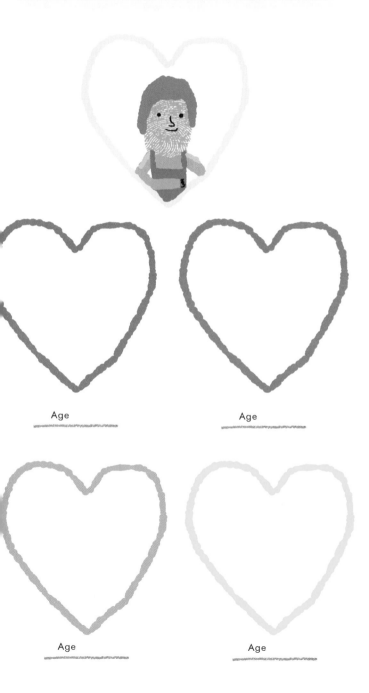

Age

Age

Age

Age

Add their name here:

Draw their portrait.

Birthday / When were your friends born?

When is their birthday date?

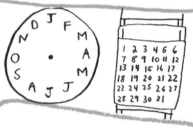

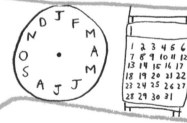

Add their name here:

Draw their portrait.

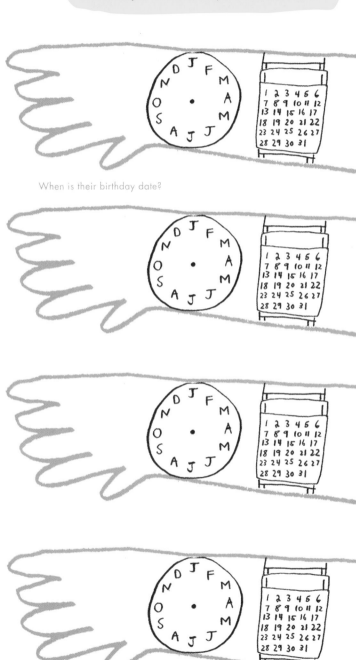

When is their birthday date?

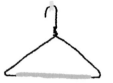

xoxo

Juan Langston Richardson II

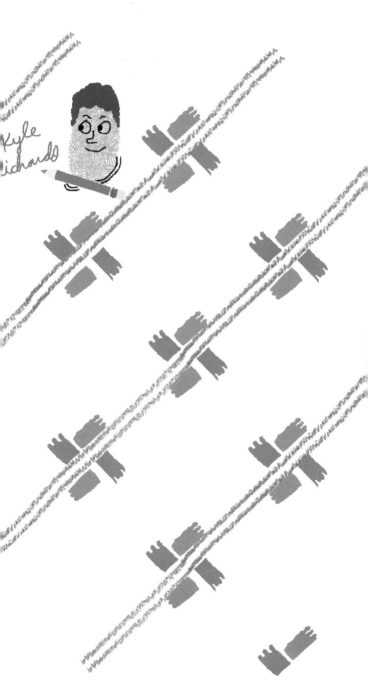

If you simplify, you amplify.

—by Bryson Vogeltanz

One kind word can warm three winter months.

Japanese proverb

Privilege is driving a smooth road and not even knowing it.

—by Ampersand (also known as Barry Deutsch)

I said to the sun, "Tell me about the big bang." The sun said, "it hurts to become."

—by Andrea Gibson,
"I Sing the Body Electric,
Especially When My Power's Out"

You are extraordinary within your limits, but your limits are extraordinary!

—by Gertrude Stein, Everybody's Autobiography

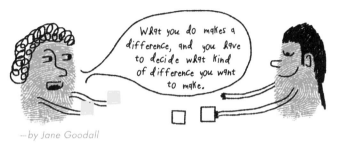

—by Jane Goodall

It takes courage to grow up and turn out to be who you really are.

—by e.e. cummings

This is a hungry lion.
You try to draw it now...

This is a bitty mouse.

This is a sitting fox.
You try to draw it now...

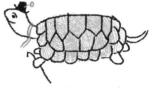

This is a fancy turtle.

This is a Chihuahua.

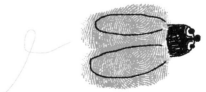

This is a flying bug.

This is a joyful
jellyfish.

You try to draw it now...

This is a sleepy sheep.

This is a dear deer.

This is a rainbow rabbit.
You try to draw it now...

This is a super skunk.

This is a merry
manatee.

This is a hot lava fireball.

You try to draw it now...

This is a spiked stilmonk.
You try to draw it now...

This is a sticky string
ball death trap.

This is a barbed bipercuda.

This is a toxic gas vapor.

You try to draw it now...

Joan Jett &
the Blackhearts

Janis Joplin
1943–1970

A visual artist

An environmental engineer

Pets / What pets did you have growing up? Do you have pets now?

Peppy Schwartz

Roger Ruby

THUMBPRINT-A-DAY

A daily diary in thumbprints.

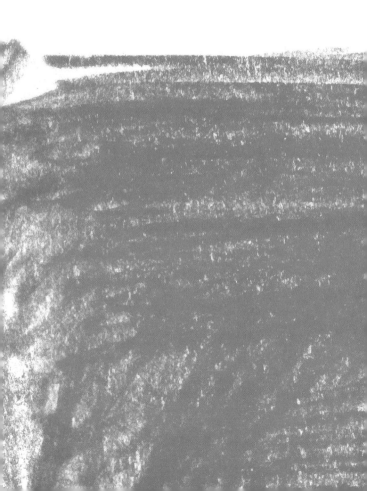

Every Day / Thumbprint portraits of how I looked
and felt each day this month.

Sun	Mon	Tues	Wed

Thurs	Fri	Sat	

Every Day / Thumbprint portraits of how I looked
and felt each day this month.

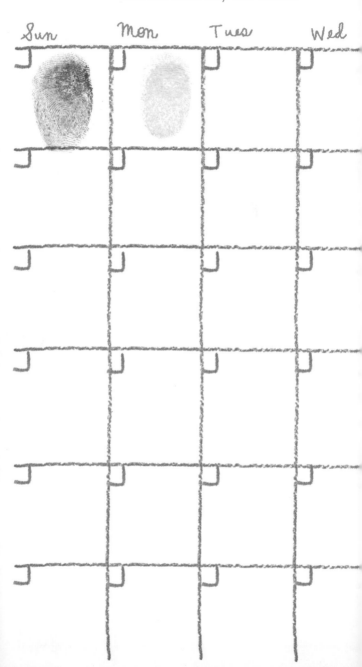

Sun	Mon	Tues	Wed

FEBRUARY

Thurs	Fri	Sat	

Every Day / Thumbprint portraits of how I looked
and felt each day this month.

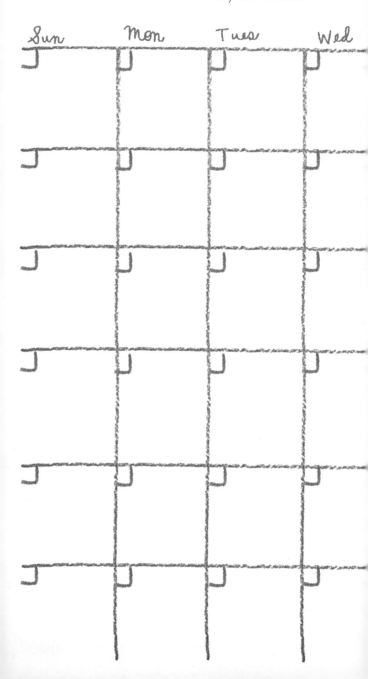

Sun	Mon	Tues	Wed

Thurs	Fri	Sat	

Every Day / Thumbprint portraits of how I looked
and felt each day this month.

Sun	Mon	Tues	Wed

APRIL

Thurs	Fri	Sat	

Every Day / Thumbprint portraits of how I looked
and felt each day this month.

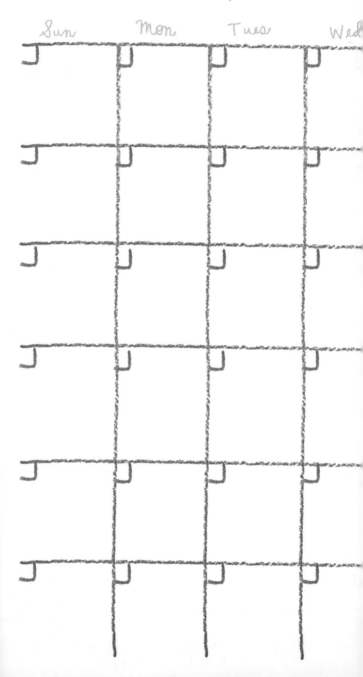

Sun	Mon	Tues	Wed

Thurs   Fri   Sat

Every Day / Thumbprint portraits of how I looked
and felt each day this month.

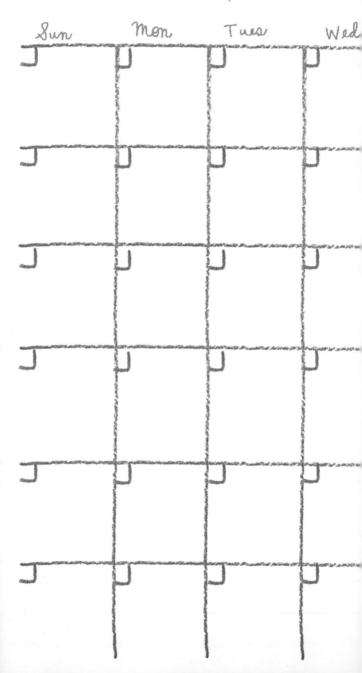

Sun	Mon	Tues	Wed

Thurs	Fri	Sat	

Every Day / Thumbprint portraits of how I looked
and felt each day this month.

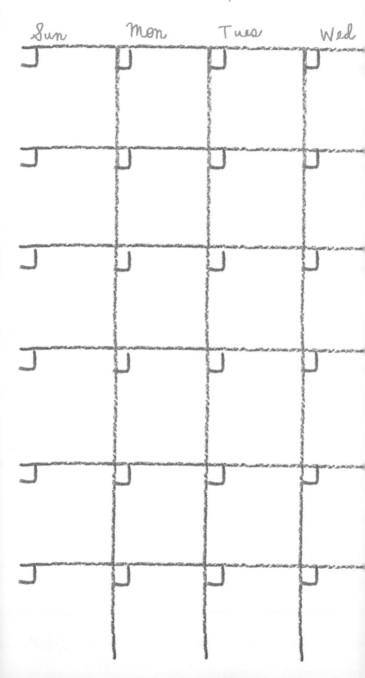

Sun	Mon	Tues	Wed

JULY

Thurs	Fri	Sat	

Every Day / Thumbprint portraits of how I looked
and felt each day this month.

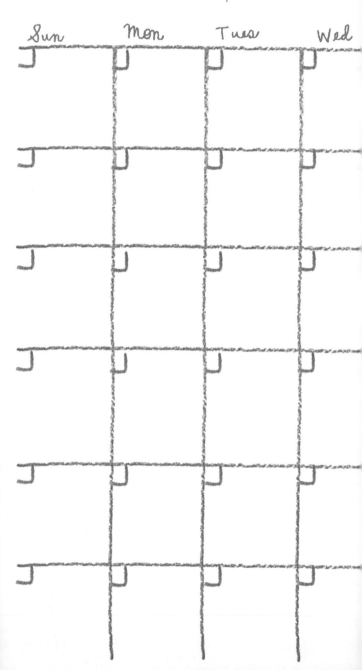

Sun	Mon	Tues	Wed

Thurs   Fri   Sat

Every Day / Thumbprint portraits of how I looked and felt each day this month.

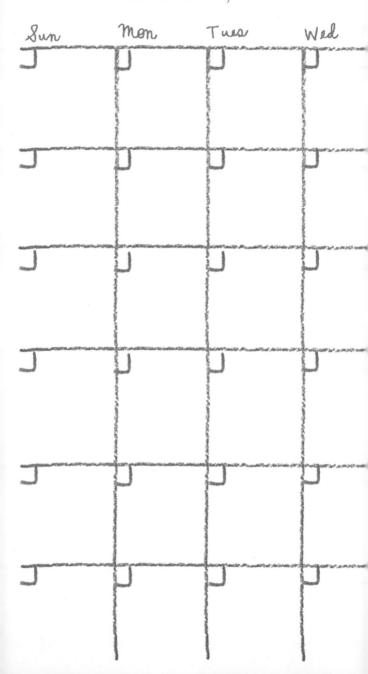

Sun	Mon	Tues	Wed

Thurs

Fri

Sat

Every Day / Thumbprint portraits of how I looked
and felt each day this month.

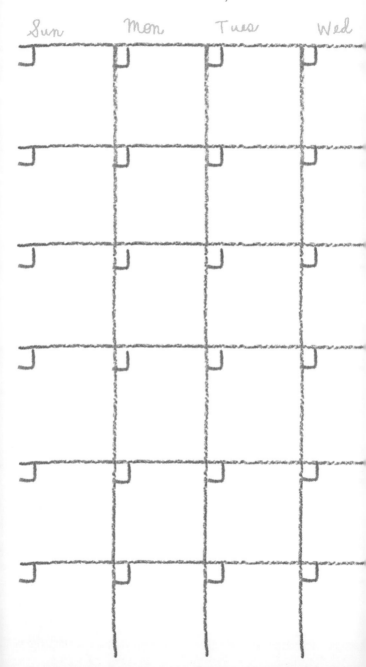

Sun	Mon	Tues	Wed

Thurs   Fri   Sat

Every Day / Thumbprint portraits of how I looked
and felt each day this month.

Sun	Mon	Tues	Wed

NOVEMBER

Thurs   Fri   Sat

Every Day / Thumbprint portraits of how I looked
and felt each day this month.

Sun	Mon	Tues	Wed

Thurs	Fri	Sat	

HAPPY NOTES

A weekly list of happy things.

Weekly / Happy people to see, places to be,
and things to remember.

Sunday, ...

Monday, ...

Tuesday, ...

Wednesday, ...

Thursday, ...

Friday, ...

Saturday, ...

Weekly / Happy people to see, places to be,
and things to remember.

Sunday, ...

Monday, ...

Tuesday, ...

Wednesday, ...

Thursday, ...

Friday, ...

Saturday, ...

Month: 1 2 3 4 5 6 7 8 9 10 11 1

Weekly / Happy people to see, places to be,
and things to remember.

Sunday, ...

Monday, ...

Tuesday, ...

Wednesday, ...

Thursday, ...

Friday, ...

Saturday, ...

Weekly / Happy people to see, places to be,
and things to remember.

Sunday, ...

Monday, ...

Tuesday, ...

Wednesday, ...

Thursday, ...

Friday, ...

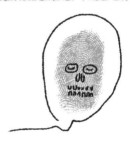

Saturday, ...

Weekly / Happy people to see, places to be,
and things to remember.

Sunday, ...

Monday, ...

Tuesday, ...

ednesday, ...

thursday, ...

riday, ...

aturday, ...

Weekly / Happy people to see, places to be,
and things to remember.

Sunday, ...

Monday, ...

Tuesday, ...

ednesday, ...

hursday, ...

riday, ...

aturday, ...

Month: 1 2 3 4 5 6 7 8 9 10 11 1

Weekly / Happy people to see, places to be,
and things to remember.

Sunday, ...

Monday, ...

Tuesday, ...

edneoday, ...

hursday, ...

riday, ...

aturday, ...

Weekly / Happy people to see, places to be,
and things to remember.

Sunday, ...

Monday, ...

Tuesday, ...

Wednesday, ...

Thursday, ...

Friday, ...

Saturday, ...

Weekly / Happy people to see, places to be,
and things to remember.

Sunday, ...

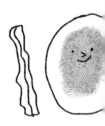

Monday, ...

Tuesday, ...

Wednesday,......................

Thursday,......................

Friday,......................

Saturday,......................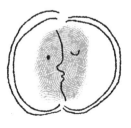

Weekly / Happy people to see, places to be,
and things to remember.

Sunday, ...

Monday, ...

Tuesday, ...

ednesday, ...

hursday, ...

riday, ...

saturday, ...

Weekly / Happy people to see, places to be,
and things to remember.

Sunday, ...

Monday, ...

Tuesday, ...

Wednesday, ...

Thursday, ...

Friday, ...

Saturday, ...

Weekly / Happy people to see, places to be,
and things to remember.

Sunday, ...

Monday, ...

Tuesday, ...

Wednesday, ...

Thursday, ...

Friday, ...

Saturday, ...

Weekly / Happy people to see, places to be,
and things to remember.

Sunday, ...

Monday, ...

Tuesday, ...

Wednesday, ...

Thursday, ...

Friday, ...

Saturday, ...

Month: 1 2 3 4 5 6 7 8 9 10 11 1

Weekly / Happy people to see, places to be,
and things to remember.

Sunday, ...

Monday, ...

Tuesday, ...

Wednesday, ...

Thursday, ...

Friday, ...

Saturday, ...

Weekly / Happy people to see, places to be,
and things to remember.

Sunday, ...

Monday, ...

Tuesday, ...

ednesday, ...

hursday, ...

riday, ...

aturday, ...

Month: 1 2 3 4 5 6 7 8 9 10 11

Weekly / Happy people to see, places to be,
and things to remember.

Sunday, ...

Monday, ...

Tuesday, ...

ednesday, ...

hursday, ...

riday, ...

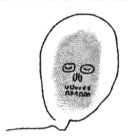

aturday, ...

Weekly / Happy people to see, places to be,
and things to remember.

Sunday, ...

Monday, ...

Tuesday, ...

ednesday, ...

hursday, ...

riday, ...

aturday, ...

Weekly / Happy people to see, places to be,
and things to remember.

Sunday, ...

Monday, ...

Tuesday, ...

WEEKLY

ednesday, ...

hursday, ...

riday, ...

aturday, ...

Weekly / Happy people to see, places to be,
and things to remember.

Sunday, ...

Monday, ...

Tuesday, ...

Wednesday, ...

Thursday, ...

Friday, ...

Saturday, ...

Month: 1 2 3 4 5 6 7 8 9 10 11 1

Weekly / Happy people to see, places to be,
and things to remember.

Sunday, ...

Monday, ...

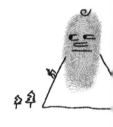

Tuesday, ...

Wednesday, ...

Thursday, ...

Friday, ...

Saturday, ...

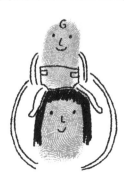

Weekly / Happy people to see, places to be,
and things to remember.

Sunday, ...

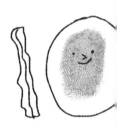

Monday, ...

Tuesday, ...

Wednesday, ...

Thursday, ...

Friday, ...

Saturday, ...

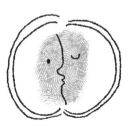

Weekly / Happy people to see, places to be,
and things to remember.

Sunday, ...

Monday, ...

Tuesday, ...

Wednesday, ...

Thursday, ...

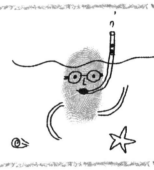

Friday, ...

Saturday, ...

Weekly / Happy people to see, places to be,
and things to remember.

Sunday, ...

Monday, ...

Tuesday, ...

WEEKLY

ednesday, ...

hursday, ...

riday, ...

aturday, ...

Weekly / Happy people to see, places to be,
and things to remember.

Sunday, ...

Monday, ...

Tuesday, ...

Wednesday,............

Thursday,............

Friday,............

Saturday,............

Month: 1 2 3 4 5 6 7 8 9 10 11 1

Weekly / Happy people to see, places to be, and things to remember.

Sunday, ...

Monday, ...

Tuesday, ...

ednesday, ...

hursday, ...

riday, ...

aturday, ...

Month: 1 2 3 4 5 6 7 8 9 10 11 1

Weekly / Happy people to see, places to be,
and things to remember.

Sunday, ...

Monday, ...

Tuesday, ...

Wednesday,.................

Thursday,.................

Friday,....................

Saturday,...............

Month: 1 2 3 4 5 6 7 8 9 10 11 1

Weekly / Happy people to see, places to be,
and things to remember.

Sunday, ...

Monday, ...

Tuesday, ...

Wednesday,............

Thursday,............

Friday,............

Saturday,............

Month: 1 2 3 4 5 6 7 8 9 10 11 1

Weekly / Happy people to see, places to be,
and things to remember.

Sunday, ...

Monday, ...

Tuesday, ...

ednesday, ...

hursday, ...

riday, ...

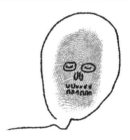

aturday, ...

Weekly / Happy people to see, places to be,
and things to remember.

Sunday, ...

Monday, ...

Tuesday, ...

ednesday,

hursday,

riday,

aturday,

Weekly / Happy people to see, places to be,
and things to remember.

Sunday, ...

Monday, ...

Tuesday, ...

ednesday, ...

hursday, ...

riday, ...

aturday, ...

Month: 1 2 3 4 5 6 7 8 9 10 11 |

Weekly / Happy people to see, places to be,
and things to remember.

Sunday, ...

Monday, ...

Tuesday, ...

ednesday, ...

hursday, ...

riday, ...

aturday, ...

Weekly / Happy people to see, places to be,
and things to remember.

Sunday, ...

Monday, ...

Tuesday, ...

Wednesday, ...

Thursday, ...

Friday, ...

Saturday, ...

Month: 1 2 3 4 5 6 7 8 9 10 11 12

Weekly / Happy people to see, places to be,
and things to remember.

Sunday, ...

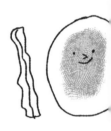

Monday, ...

Tuesday, ...

Wednesday, ...

Thursday, ...

Friday, ...

Saturday, ...

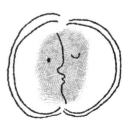

Month: 1 2 3 4 5 6 7 8 9 10 11 1[

Weekly / Happy people to see, places to be,
and things to remember.

Sunday, ...

Monday, ...

Tuesday, ...

ednesday, ...

hursday, ...

riday, ...

aturday, ...

Month: 1 2 3 4 5 6 7 8 9 10 11 12

Weekly / Happy people to see, places to be,
and things to remember.

Sunday, ...

Monday, ...

Tuesday, ...

ednesday,................

hursday,................

riday,................

aturday,................

Weekly / Happy people to see, places to be, and things to remember.

Sunday,...............

Monday,...............

Tuesday,...............

ednesday,........................

hursday,........................

riday,........................

aturday,........................

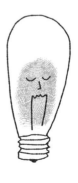

Weekly / Happy people to see, places to be,
and things to remember.

Sunday, ...

Monday, ...

Tuesday, ...

ednesday, ...

ursday, ...

iday, ...

turday, ...

Month: 1 2 3 4 5 6 7 8 9 10 11

Weekly / Happy people to see, places to be,
and things to remember.

Sunday, ...

Monday, ...

Tuesday, ...

ednesday, ...

hursday, ...

riday, ...

aturday, ...

Month: 1 2 3 4 5 6 7 8 9 10 11 1

Weekly / Happy people to see, places to be,
and things to remember.

Sunday, ...

Monday, ...

Tuesday, ...

Wednesday, ...

Thursday, ...

Friday, ...

Saturday, ...

Weekly / Happy people to see, places to be,
and things to remember.

Sunday, ...

Monday, ...

Tuesday, ...

Wednesday, ...

Thursday, ...

Friday, ...

Saturday, ...

Weekly / Happy people to see, places to be,
and things to remember.

Sunday, ...

Monday, ...

Tuesday, ...

Wednesday, ...

Thursday, ...

Friday, ...

Saturday, ...

Weekly / Happy people to see, places to be,
and things to remember.

Sunday, ...

Monday, ...

Tuesday, ...

Wednesday, ...

Thursday, ...

Friday, ...

Saturday, ...

Weekly / Happy people to see, places to be,
and things to remember.

Sunday, ...

Monday, ...

Tuesday, ...

Wednesday................

Thursday................

Friday................

Saturday................

Weekly / Happy people to see, places to be,
and things to remember.

Sunday, ...

Monday, ...

Tuesday, ...

WEEKLY

ednesday, ...

hursday, ...

riday, ...

aturday, ...

Weekly / Happy people to see, places to be,
and things to remember.

Sunday, ...

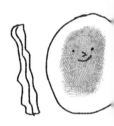

Monday, ...

Tuesday, ...

WEEKLY

ednesday, ...

hursday, ...

riday, ...

aturday, ...

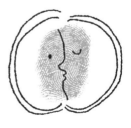

Weekly / Happy people to see, places to be,
and things to remember.

Sunday, ...

Monday, ...

Tuesday, ...

ednesday, ...

hursday, ...

riday, ...

aturday, ...

Weekly / Happy people to see, places to be,
and things to remember.

Sunday, ...

Monday, ...

Tuesday, ...

Wednesday, ...

Thursday, ...

Friday, ...

Saturday, ...

Month: 1 2 3 4 5 6 7 8 9 10 11 1

Weekly / Happy people to see, places to be,
and things to remember.

Sunday,....................

Monday,....................

Tuesday,....................

WEEKLY

Wednesday, ...

Thursday, ...

Friday, ...

Saturday, ...

Weekly / Happy people to see, places to be,
and things to remember.

Sunday, ...

Monday, ...

Tuesday, ...

Wednesday, ...

Thursday, ...

Friday, ...

Saturday, ...

Month: 1 2 3 4 5 6 7 8 9 10 11 1

Weekly / Happy people to see, places to be,
and things to remember.

Sunday, ...

Monday, ...

Tuesday, ...

Wednesday, ...

Thursday, ...

Friday, ...

Saturday, ...

Weekly / Happy people to see, places to be,
and things to remember.

Sunday, ...

Monday, ...

Tuesday, ...

Wednesday, ...

Thursday, ...

Friday, ...

Saturday, ...

Month: 1 2 3 4 5 6 7 8 9 10 11

Weekly / Happy people to see, places to be,
and things to remember.

Sunday, ...

Monday, ...

Tuesday, ...

Wednesday,........................

Thursday,........................

Friday,........................

Saturday,........................

Weekly / Happy people to see, places to be,
and things to remember.

Sunday, ...

Monday, ...

Tuesday, ...

ednesday, ...

hursday, ...

riday, ...

aturday, ...